Credo for the Checkout Line in Winter

With *Credo for the Checkout Line in Winter,* Maryann Corbett offers us yet another beautifully crafted group of poems deploying formal technique but linguistically and thematically inventive. Corbett is as comfortable and affecting within the tight confines of the Old English alliterative meter ("Cold Case") and the Sapphic stanza ("Paint Store") as she is with her supple blank verse and terza rima. Yet never does her rigorous craft interfere with the thoughtful, insightful content of these poems. A stunning collection, from one of America's most gifted contemporary poets.
—Marilyn L. Taylor

What makes Maryann Corbett such a rare, excellent writer must be her talent for weaving together various artistic impulses, so that her poems often sound both traditional and brand new, both humorous and serious, both worldly-wise and, as John Keats once put it, "capable of being in uncertainties." [She] remains a poet of the first order, and her poems are cause for gratitude, and deep enjoyment.
—Peter Campion (full text in the foreword)

The crafted poems in Maryann Corbett's new book are vibrant. She is a newborn Robert Frost, with a wicked eye for contemporary life. Each poem surprises. I like to discover about the moon that at "Seven a.m. The hunter's moon/ a scarface falling down the sky/ in knife-edge dark. A siren sounds/ its bad-suspense-film leitmotif." Trees, gardens, awkward paradises move into the poems as does the lyric "Chiller" which ends strongly with "The dead hand of a pin-oak leaf/ crabwalks across the alleyway." Read her poems and feel the howling snow, the mud, and the jubilance of the first warm fertile spring days.
—Willis Barnstone

Do not dismiss this collection as "domestic poetry," "women's verse." Though grounded in seasonal rhythms and familiar settings, it is as vigorous, as reflective, as important as any man's. Sharply visual, skillfully and cleverly crafted, her poems draw out essences, "concentrated" and persisting. "Beauty changes us,/ calling up wonder from our deepest selves/ to its right place."

    —Catharine Savage Brosman

These masterful poems announce themselves as winter pieces, and indeed they are so full of sleet and snow that readers may wish to dress warmly. But Corbett's winter, a season when "dull forms come in the mail" and we eat "tasteless, stone-hard, gassed tomatoes," is always lushly haunted by the other seasons, the way a house in one of her poems is fronted by a "three-season porch." Summers and autumns past are "held in suspension" by memory (and by jars of dried rose petals, their "complexities still fragrant on the air"), and the looming "two-faced spring" is bodied forth by hope ("I believe with perfect faith/ in the rounded, fragrant heirloom types to come") and by fear—or rather by the knowledge that, spring or not, for us as for the beautiful Dutch Elms in another poem, "in every year, some go." Corbett is one of the best-kept secrets of American poetry, and this is one of the best new collections I've read in years.

    —Geoffrey Brock

CREDO *for the* CHECKOUT LINE *in* WINTER

POEMS BY
Maryann Corbett

ABLE MUSE PRESS

Printed in the United States of America

Library of Congress Control Number: 2013932424

ISBN 978-1-927409-14-5 (paperback)
ISBN 978-1-927409-15-2 (digital)

Cover image: "Farewell" by Ivana Bruteničová

Cover & book design by Alexander Pepple

Able Muse Press is an imprint of *Able Muse:* A Review of Poetry, Prose & Art—at www.ablemuse.com

Able Muse Press
467 Saratoga Avenue #602
San Jose, CA 95129

For John

"This suspense is terrible. I hope it will last."

— Oscar Wilde

Acknowledgments

I am grateful to the editors of the following journals where many of these poems originally appeared, sometimes in earlier versions.

14 by 14: "Institute of Art, Spring Break."

Able Muse: "Weather Radio."

Alabama Literary Review: "Airheads," "Light, Motif."

Anglican Theological Review: "Ballade for the Last Move."

Astropoetica: "Saving the Appearances."

Birmingham Poetry Review: "Soundtrack."

The Chimaera: "Cold Case," "Feast of Corpus Christi," "Mayday," "Pea Planting, Good Friday."

Chronicles: "Life Bird," "Rose Catalogue in January," "The Videographer's Beethoven."

Horizon Review: "Holiday Concert," "Incident Report," "Portent."

Italian Americana: "A Theory of Gardens in the Second Generation."

Linebreak: "Two Funerals."

Loch Raven Review: "Layover."

The Lyric: "Chiller," "Dutch Elm."

Mezzo Cammin: "The Art Student's Mother Thinks Out Loud," "Cuttings."

Poemeleon: "Maintenance Work."

Poetry Revolt: "Viva Voce."

The Raintown Review: "After the Divorce, I Hold a Yard Sale," "Phone Call, 6:00 A.M."

Relief: "Front-Page Photograph, Memorial Day."

Rock and Sling: "Confessional Work: Late Advent."

Ruminate: "Late Season Day Trip."

The Shit Creek Review: "Emergences," "Seeing Women in Hijab, the Businesswoman Thinks about Fabric," "Vintage Pattern."

Snakeskin: "Epistle to the Pumpkin Field."

Soundzine: "Paint Store."

Terrain: "After Epiphany: Side Street," "Credo for the Checkout Line in Winter," "Terzanelle for the Pilgrimage to Rosedale."

Think Journal: "Finding the Lego."

Umbrella: "Express."

Verse Wisconsin: "A Choral Service for All Souls."

Wake: "Preservation."

Four of the poems appeared in the chapbook *Gardening in a Time of War* (Pudding House, 2007), and four appeared in the chapbook *Dissonance* (Scienter Press, 2009). "Rose Catalogue in January" appeared in the anthology *Hot Sonnets* (Entasis Press, 2011).

My warmest thanks to Alex Pepple, and to the poets, administrators, and staff of *Eratosphere, Sonnet Central,* and *The Roundup* for their comments on many of these poems.

Since first encountering Maryann Corbett's poems, I've wondered: what makes them so impressive and so poignant? Is it the poet's consummate formal skill, her ability to set phrases and lines in dynamic relation, so that each syllable feels inevitable? Or is it her insouciant yet sympathetic wit? How about her magician's knack for conjuring places, people and feeling-tones, in a few, seemingly spontaneous strokes?

I suspect the answer is: all of the above. What makes Maryann Corbett such a rare, excellent writer must be her talent for weaving together various artistic impulses, so that her poems often sound both traditional and brand new, both humorous and serious, both worldly-wise and, as John Keats once put it, "capable of being in uncertainties."

Consider the first three quatrains of "Paint Store":

> Stand there, stunned and gawking, before these altars:
> walls of flapping prayer-flags with names like poems.
> What might happen? Glamours and transformations.
> Pasts disappearing:

teal, vermilion, ultramarine. You drink them,
suck them in like opiates. Choose them wildly.
Wield them. Then the walls in your head might crack their
cipher of blankness—

Choice, though. Walling in at a single vision.
Sinking in it. Painting it into corners.
Once, you did it: namings and nursery colors.
Emily. Yellow.

The first thing I noticed when I read these lines was their unique tone, their blend of the mundane and the otherworldly. Corbett writes in a high lyrical register of "Glamours and transformations" and of the Romantic imperative to "Choose them wildly." But the poem never abandons the reality of hardware store. The humor of "stunned and gawking" and the biographical aside about "namings and nursery colors" remind us that, at least in the world of these superb poems, our glamours and transformations occur in the so-called "ordinary" lives we lead with others, among our work, our family lives, even our domestic repairs.

In fact, the refusal of false dualities seems characteristic of Corbett. Her great concern in *Credo for the Checkout Line in Winter* is the integration of the ritual and the day-to-day. As the title suggests, this book is about finding what to believe in, and honoring those beliefs, even while accepting a healthy dose of skepticism. This simultaneous faith in both the here-and-now and the beyond allows the paint cans to be both "prayer flags" and, well, paint cans.

It took me a couple re-readings before I realized another marvelous aspect of "Paint Store." The poem is in sapphics, the notoriously difficult form, named after the great Ancient Greek poet, who used the form for her own odes of ritual address, of spiritual and worldly longing. Certainly, Corbett's management of the form is commendable—masterful, even. But what impresses me most is not that she has plucked some gold ring from the carrousel of rhyme and meter. Rather, it's the lack of any boast or "see here": Corbett's sapphics course beneath the sounds of her American English with ease and grace. They are as amenable to her voice as—so we discover in these same lines—the ritual impulse is to a day of errands.

I could point to other such instances of Corbett's integration of formal skill and spiritual scope. Take, for example, the terza rima tercets of "Maintenance Work." Or consider the beautiful sonnets "Soundtrack" and "Phone Call, 6 A.M."

But perhaps the best thing would be to turn the pages here, and delve deeply into these poems themselves. I can think of few poets who address the whole range of modern experience with such a thoroughly felt, and personal, understanding of poetic history. Maryann Corbett remains a poet of the first order, and her poems are cause for gratitude, and deep enjoyment.

—Peter Campion

Contents

III

IV

Credo for the Checkout Line in Winter

I

Terzanelle for the Pilgrimage
to Rosedale

A ritual for the year about to turn:
we drive off, ceremonious, under a dark
star-pricked and clear. A tinsel-curl of moon

fades in floodlight over the lots. We park
close in, the early wisps of a winter storm
driving the ceremony. Under the dark

of doubt and terrible headlines, let us perform
to oboe sounds, in ice-lights, a mime of hope.
The midweek lull, false calm before the storm,

and the mild Mozart soothe. Can this lightscape
lay the old ghosts of children's fallen faces?
Can ice-lights, oboes, dissipate the fog-shape

of errors past, or futures with hollow voices
that bark, saluting, *Nothing to report—*?
Well, let us hope. Let us stroll with lifted faces

and cleave to sound and ceremony and art,
in rituals for a year about to turn
dark corners. Space is flinging itself apart
star-pricked and clear, with a tinsel-curl of moon.

Confessional Work: Late Advent

Long lines at this season, everywhere.
I'm used to them: airport security,
checkout, post office queue, holiday movie.
In darkness that falls early, they fold into corners,
hugging the buildings for something like support.

Always the choreography of burden,
balanced against the hip, hugged to the chest,
kicked ahead of me in the snaking line:
the carry-on that I already know
will not fit in the overhead compartment,
the package that can never arrive by Christmas
to buy me an impossible absolution,
the near-despair clutched at for thirty years,
the pointless sin, the life I never fix—
when my arms tire, I will drag it across the floor
through a trail of puddle left by slushy boots
to a counter where a face, with practiced patience,
will ask me, *Anything else?* and motion me on.

And all this longing for no reason I know,
except that even now, the lumped gray sky—
as if it heard earth sing *Rorate coeli*—
plops down fat flakes, thick with springlike wetness,
and parking lots filled with the scraps of autumn
look cleaner, in the very way we beg for
in the prayer of another season: *white as snow.*

Holiday Concert

Forgive us. We have dragged them into the night
in taffeta dresses, in stiff collars and ties,
with the wind damp, the sleet raking their cheeks,

to school lunchrooms fitted with makeshift stages
where we will sit under bad fluorescent lighting
on folding chairs, and they will sing and play.

We will watch the first grader with little cymbals,
bending her knees, hunched in concentration
while neighbors snicker at her ardent face.

Forgive us. We will hear the seventh-grade boy
as his voice finally loses its innocence
forever, at the unbearable solo moment

and know that now, for years, he will wince at the thought
of singing, yet will ache to sing, in silence,
silence even to the generation to come

with its night, its sleet, its hideous lunchroom chairs.

The Videographer's Beethoven

"Bliss was it in that dawn to be alive,
But to be young was very heaven. . . ."
  – William Wordsworth

An anthill making music—
from the second balcony, all my aging eyes
see of the Ninth's last outburst from so many student bodies,
the twenty bow-arms back in furious rebellion.

But someone else's vision
informs the sound. On screens that flank the proscenium,
single faces: a tenor's eyebrows, lifted
amazed, to Schiller's canopy of stars.

If the eye draws back to the stage,
the ear succumbs to the sweep of the *millionen*
who blare in battle formation,
in the long view, in the hard synthetic light.
And sometimes a lone hero, his cymbals a lifted shimmer.

But this is mythmaking. Fact
is the close, the sidelong seeing
                    of someone who knows these measures:
the curls on a cellist's neck, her upswept hair
losing its inhibitions
                    in the *kiss of the whole world,*

the flame-haired soprano, unfolding
meanings for *feuertrunken.*

Brüder! they sing, as the camera
pans the perfect faith of their major chord,
then *Brüder!* again, more softly,
shifting in the lower voices

to resignation the screen reveals in their eyes,
already learning, I think, to temper their hopes,
knowing how history goes—
these new Romantics, beginning their long decline.

Northeast Digs Out from Record Snowfall

All up and down the coast, where Saturday
a generous snow came down, an ancient magic
appears this morning: every hack reporter
in every local rag now lifts the lyre
in lieu of pad and pencil. In New York,
it is a *milk-white morning;* snow transforms
the *straw-drab landscapes into winter postcards.*
Southward the mood is darker: *like a cloak*
of madness falls the snow, *like one of those*
quiet obsessions you read about in stories.
Figure and trope and image sift, drift over
the dailiness of the papers. Even where
the gods are feebler, on the weather page,
the lyric muse now takes the words by storm:
fierce winds and *dazzling whiteness, thigh-deep drifts,*
adjectives blowing thick and piling fast,
and under everything the sonorous meter
of radios intoning cancellations.
Those few lost souls with no poetic spark
wander the parks and murmur, staring upward,
"so quiet" and *"so lovely,"* and their awe
is duly reported, being perhaps the news
most worth reporting: beauty changes us,
calling up wonder from our deepest selves
to its right place, page one, above the fold.

Rose Catalogue in January

You want them, yes, the year's new hybrid teas,
long-stemmed, high-centered, pointed, budded tight.
You hesitate at old varieties'
neediness, at fogs of pesticide,
thorny defenses, sensitivities—

But close your eyes. Think how you loved them once,
those hundred-petalled secrecies within
Fantin-Latour, those foldings, sinuous, dense.
Think of rugosa petals' openness,
of rounded hips that bore the weight of winter,

and albas: how their breathings stir the past.
How essence, concentrated, will persist
when nothing's left but fragments in a jar,
complexities still fragrant on the air.

Express

In snow, in darkness, we wait for the 53.
It plods up Marshall under the meager streetlights,
its tires spattering curbs with a slurry of gray.
Aboard, we sink into ourselves, our papers,
our thick-down-jacket armor against the world,
the way the bus drops down the on-ramp's incline
to bore down I-94.
              Outside, blackness;
inside, eerily bright, like Hopper's diner
hurtling along at sixty miles an hour,
everyone's eyes as private as if we wore
those gray fedoras. Sleuthing, we hunt for answers
while brilliant necklace beads of westward headlight
string themselves toward us, past us, in the dark.

A shift of light: we're into the labyrinth
where on- and off-ramps knit with city streets,
over and under. And now instead we're like
the crews on submarines in old war movies:
cramped, quiet, sunk in the interstate's ocean—
moving as if in a thousand feet of water,
weighed down by the weather forecast—twenty below—
the headline that says the local Guard battalion
will have its tour extended, the news that life
will go on as it has. At the Fifth Street exit,
we surface to globes and twinkles: Winter Carnival

set to go on in spite of everything.
Now one block at a time: stop go stop go.
We dribble off, dispersing like the photons,
kept going only by the laws of physics.
Nothing here bears witness to the light
but a stain bleeding into the eastern sky.

Cold Case

They're less than clear,

     the clues you look through,

but bode no good.

     The bent needles.

The crystal glass.

     Crackhead glyphs—

obscure, a script

     in a screwball scrawl—

craze the surfaces,

     streaking symbols

in drugged frenzy,

     all dendrites firing.

Blinking's no good.

     What blurs your vision

has deeper roots:

     the years of damage.

The sheer pain

     you've been staring past,

stumped. But take

     a stab at a name.

After Epiphany: Side Street

A leaden matins. Up the block,
the scattered crows voice disapproval.
A tow truck groans: someone has fallen victim
to the hard machinery of snow removal.

Someone has fallen, hard. The alley
lies there plotting its slick betrayal.
Fog-freeze blears my prospects. Time ticks dully,
keeping accounts. Dull forms come in the mail.

Fallen on ordinary time,
I drag the stripped tree to the trash,
struggling along a straight-and-narrow climb.
The roadside snow takes on the grit of ash,

quits with the season, glum, half gray.
Salted by sober reckoning,
I hunker down, not ready yet to pay
the debt of penance for another spring.

Credo for the Checkout Line
in Winter

Even while sleet spits in the parking lot
and a bored girl with a tongue stud and fuchsia hair
rings up these tasteless, stone-hard, gassed tomatoes,
even now, I believe with perfect faith
in the rounded, fragrant heirloom types to come.
In covered farmers' markets where flats of pansies
spread in uncountable rows, their petals trembling
all over,
        exactly the way it felt once, new-
shucked from tux and tulle, sprung from our childhoods,
rocketing into new lives, our possessions
wagging behind us, crammed in a twelve-foot U-Haul
with a governor and no radio, belting John Denver
at the tops of our lungs for eleven hundred miles
of farmland stippled green.
                And on the third day
we came, gravel-throated and bone-jarred,
to the place appointed. A stony hole in the ground
gaped where a street should go, in front of our building,
and we lugged our laden dressers across the blocks
through air gritty with seasonal road construction,
not faltering even then. And forty years
of falling on stony ground still see us springing
for Aprils,
       and therefore I believe in the future

of the geeky bagger who never meets my eyes
but will someday win the smile of the pink-haired cashier.
In palms, as they beckon to me from glossy covers
and sway over swimwear that conquers the laws of physics.
In Elvis, who will return in a blaze of sequins
to burn away all sorrow, yea though he tarry.

II

Emergences

"Nothing is so beautiful as spring."
– *Gerard Manley Hopkins*

The mud sucks up the filthy snow
and swallows. From the shrunken mass
the bus-stop beer cans crown and grow.
A season's meanness dots the grass.
We wait; we wait. The weather breaks.
It heaves the bones of old mistakes:

where gulls pick trash from parking lots
and dandelions brood the seed
set to subvert our garden plots,
we pick our poisons weed by weed
and plan. We plan; we never learn
these are the tricks the seasons turn

while down the alleys' potholed lines,
through muscled-open windows come
the mower-motors' manic whines
and street rods at the stoplight hum
hard vices in their deepest throats,
decades-old discordant notes,

menace we never quite forget.
We wait. We are not younger yet.

Cuttings

A sort of birthday poem for my daughter

Late-winter labor, long without progressing
and hard. At last, the C-section, and you.
A card and giddy flowers from my sister—
Dutch iris, jonquils. Wands of pussywillow.

Hopeless sucker for any dream that blooms
and for quick, cut-to-the-chase relief from waiting,
I've held onto a faith in silver catkins.
That long, cold, swaddled spring, dreaming of branches
to bring indoors for forcing, I bought a shrub,
a bare two-footer in a gallon pot,
planted it and retreated. You and I
kept to the house, learning each other's rhythms,
waiting for growth to happen, as it would.
It was mud season. Alleys ran in runnels
through ice ruts, carrying wind-ripped plastic bags.

Twenty-five years. A woman with any sense
would cut it down, this proof of magical thinking
that laughed off warnings: *Grows to thirty feet.*
Its catkins, well above the roofline now,
pass tongue-stage, blown to sticky-bristled blobbets
of yellowcake. They atom-bomb my asthma.
They drop too near the house, a matted mess
clogging the gutters, fouling the ratty lawn.

I say this every year. And then the jays
and cardinals inspect the real estate
to nest, and the heart cuts back to where we started.

A Theory of Gardens
in the Second Generation

Like cutting out my tongue.
A wound, to find a new country could feel
unsayable, or false. That words were wrong

because the place was wrong. She could not say
rondine; the pronged tail
was wrongly colored, and the way

it flicked was wrong. She could pronounce
garofano; but the puff-petaled ball
was not her mountain flower, with its dance

like the small goats. So if she said to her child
garofano, rondine, the words failed.
Dropped from her lips, words tangled in the wind

unless she staked them—pinned them
tight to the plainest generality.
Uccello, bird. *Albero,* tree.

Only *il pomodoro* and *la rosa*
held true in their particulars—in the mouth, the nose:
the tart scarlet, the crimson like a bruise.

Her child, who spent his life
posing, bluffing, unsure of what he knew,
rooted himself in two
brilliant specific facts: *Tomato. Rose.*

Pea Planting, Good Friday

Air cold, and ground still stiff
as if
opened against its will,
he still
planted, with chilly care.
Were there
good reasons every year
for early setting-out?
His habits trump her doubt
as if he still were there.

The Art Student's Mother Thinks Out Loud

I can't believe you're going back to clean,
white canvas. All that work, gessoed away—
tossed, a lightweight love affair, expunged,
wiped out with giant swipes of a housepaint brush.
You swab it on in globs, a cumulus
fair weather over the storm of art that blew

out of your cloudy head. You wanted blue,
you said; you needed paint. I let you clean
me out of hallway touch-up color. In cumulous
rag piles, Pollocky drips, you slathered away
days, nights, acrylics, oils—used every brush
you own, and then took mine, down to the sponge

out of my kitchen. Stuff I let you sponge
off me, wasted! You never settle. You blow
things off. I'll stick with words instead of brushes,
chisels, cameras, things you have to clean,
maintain, replace, keep dribbling away
cash on. I'm tight: fond of accumula-

tion, hoarding, piling up (what cumulus
means: a pile). I soaked up like a sponge
my mother's Thirties ethic: *Throw away
nothing!* Yet somehow, out of the blue,
here you are, a spendthrift, prodigal, clean
break with your ancestral line, a brush

with risk and danger. Should I learn to brush
off years of ingrained habit? Rain like a cumulo-
nimbus crazy thunderhead, wring clean
this brain of words till it's an empty sponge?
Spend myself with abandon on the blue
jewel of a poem, not care what blows away?

Grasp it: the world likes waste. It throws away
a million buds from the backyard tree; we brush
them off the walks, into the compost. They blow
down freely. No resentment. White as cumulus,
your empty canvas waits to be the sponge
for your next grand inspiration. In the clean,

clean air outside, rough with the breeze's airbrush,
old work is scoured away, and cumulus-
white sponges are scrubbing off the sky's blank blue.

Institute of Art, Spring Break

A bouts-rimés on words proposed by Tony Barnstone

She's home; we hit the new exhibits. Shall I mimic
her knowing comments on the fare the galleries serve us?
She talks exalted theory; I hear *slick* and *gimmick.*
The tall white silence settles in. It makes me nervous,
her taste for the exotic, life as art and theater.
(The thrill of body piercings, hair dyed flaming red.)
The gift shop, then, as neutral zone? Perhaps I need a
book to explain it all. (Parent as chickenhead.)

But she has plans and schedules, and we need to focus.
Sunset; her bus is coming. (Am I sounding dour?)
She rattles on: world-travel plans, fresh hocus-pocus.
Off now; goodbye! New man again: ah, sweet. And sour.
The white facade, gazed back at from the transit stall,
glows pink, like grade-school posters of the Taj Mahal.

Paint Store

Stand there, stunned and gawking, before these altars:
walls of flapping prayer-flags with names like poems.
What might happen? Glamours and transformations.
Pasts disappearing:

teal, vermilion, ultramarine. You drink them,
suck them in like opiates. Choose them wildly.
Wield them. Then the walls in your head might crack their
cipher of blankness—

Choice, though. Walling in at a single vision.
Sinking in it. Painting it into corners.
Once, you did it: namings and nursery colors.
Emily. Yellow.

Now you think of walk-throughs. Of thinner spirits
shrinking from the force of these saturated
indigos and corals. A sift of ashfall.
Shifting to neutrals,

selling out to selfless release, you settle.
Beige and cream serenity. Light. *Satori.*
Hand the palette over and stare away to
ceiling-white absence.

Reservations

Maples in almost-May,
flowering chartreuse, fling
a deshabille of loose
light over curving limbs,
tossing reserve to the winds
as if they'd never heard
a line from a two-faced spring—
as if they bought it all—

while honey locust trees,
arthritic-jointed, stiff,
are standing off. They dip
the barest leafbud-tip
into the warming air,
keeping in cold control
the slow-sapped unbelief
they've hardened in since fall.

Airheads

These past few days, our local air
displays its moves with floating fuzz:
cottonwood seed *scintillulas*
accost my nostrils, haunt my hair.
They dance like Salome; they tease
with half-cracked helices of flight.
Waffling at each offered breeze,
fluff-head flecks, electron-light,
ride downdrafts like adagio rain—
the next half-second, loft again,
jumping at every chance to shirk
the settling down, the rooted work.
Bad moves, but just how I behave.
The weighty efforts that might save
my soul, my health, my solvency
I balk at, loving faddish stuff—
the fizz of tabloid and TV,
light music, frothy poetry—
composing life from airhead fluff.
No hundredfold of yield is found
from seed that never hits the ground,
so I take comfort when I see
white seed-fuzz piling up in grass,
brought down to earth by modest mass,
a ratio that pleases me:
some gravitas, much levity.

Vintage Pattern

Fitted dinner dress with bolero jacket, ca. 1963

Grasping the tidy block of folded tissue,
slip it free of its corseting envelope.
The package reads *Simplicity*. The issue

unfolds its complications. They were many:
the parts to fit, the arts in altering.
Snip the sheets into bits, the flimsy, filmy

crinkles of fragile onionskin. Then press
each piece creaselessly perfect: nothing must veer
from measure. Decades now since you have done this.

Recall the coaxing curve to curve. The pinning.
The fingers teasing all into compliance.
The maddening cling and fray of satin lining.

The stay-stitching, the trim of seams, the turn.
The whipstitch as it cinches a final closure.
The way, at last, it all reverts to pattern.

Recall this. Then pick up the length of sable,
the black depths of this present to yourself.
Spill all its luxury across the table,

six yards. Silk velvet. Think of its perfection.
How it could still be anything. And now
taking a breath, begin its vivisection.

Seeing Women in Hijab,
the Businesswoman Thinks about Fabric

The veils themselves are beautiful, no question,
and in this neighborhood they wear them long.
Fluidly draped, rich-textured, and in colors
too sumptuous for buttoned business wear,
they smooth all movement, turning simple acts,
like walking, sitting, lifting an arm, to art.
A hem off-kilter sometimes says *home-sewn*.
I notice, and think of how I used to sew.
In fact, I still waste time in fabric stores,
modest ones in the Midway, the very same
stores where Somali women shop for veiling.
I haunt the aisles of "special occasion" fabric,
drinking the varied hues and saturations—
aquamarine and celadon, wine, plum.
Evening wear was what I loved to sew,
"evening and bridal" in the pattern books.
Dances and proms and weddings, so much sewing—
But the thrill was never only the finished dress.
The thrill was the fabric—satin, crepe de chine,
silk dupioni, taffeta, organza—
the uncut rivers running off the bolt.
Roll out a bolt of velvet, you're transformed
to oriental empress. Cut it up
in little pieces for constructed garments,
you're right back to your wage-slave weekday role.

The clothes approved for Western working life
fit closely. They have no extraneous drape,
no flow, nothing to veil the daily grind.
The clothes that let you love the cloth itself—
brocaded stiffness, nuzzling velveteen,
bias-cut satin pouring over a thigh—
are evening and bridal wear, or period costumes,
with bodices and corsets that grip the waist
above a gathered skirt that opens softly
like an enormous rose, the dress of dreams,
the fabric of fantasy, like nothing at all
I wear these days, life being what it is.
The dream needs yards of fabric. Like those veils.
Which brings me back to the stabbing little needles
of questioning, when a Muslim woman's veil
brushes me as she passes in the aisle
of the 16A, as all of us ride downtown
to weekdays that are not the lives we dreamed.

Mayday

Remembering "Make Way for Ducklings"

From the small safety of their storm-drain puddle,
two bird-brained birds
puzzle across four lanes at seven a.m. They bob and waddle
—there *are* no other words—
his iridescent head, green beyond mistaking,
blazing a way for her dull brown. Unhurried,
they preen at the midline, pecking
at air. I pause mid-step beside the roadway, worried,

because my childhood faith, set on the sacred texts
read to me, read to my children, still blessing the shelves
of the branch library, holds that some love protects
such innocent selves.
It wants a policeman to materialize,
whistling and gesturing with white-gloved hands.
Slim chance: in less benevolent guise,
he stands

above with radar gun, in dark blue interdiction
while cars bomb down the pavement toward our couple, forty-fiving
in a thirty zone. The gods of children's fiction
appear not to be driving
this plot.
        (Do I expect them to hold sway,

or the grown-ups' god, the Stillness in the Dance?
The Ground of Being, who let the ground give way
in Port-au-Prince?

Two bobbing question marks.)
Above the creeping-charlie's faultless blue,
a chalk-white smudge of contrail arcs
across a sky by Watteau. Everything stills.
                                        For now,
driver-attention holds, and brakes are firm and good.
Ducks cross in danger and care, those ancient, storied laws.
Early light spangles the cottonwood.
A flowering crab confettis its applause.

Life Bird

Acadian flycatcher reported at Bass Ponds, June 29

Sightings. Clipped reports of an observation
here or there, an as-it-is-written signal.
Likelier, a voice—like Elijah's: tiny
whistling sounds. The postings begin appearing.
Here. No, *there.* The gatherings start, the eager
grayhead old, binocular-necked, all-knowing.

Huddled on a path in a wetland clearing,
conferencing: has anyone really heard it?
There again, that call. Do their ears mislead them,
hardened, unaccustomed to visitations?
No, it's there. The life bird, the one they wait for,
silent, rapt (think Fatima, Medjugorje).

Red-winged blackbird buzzing, with bullfrog accents,
flashing orange shoulders above the cattails;
yellow warblers; barn swallows; iridescent
dragonflies in aquamarine and turquoise;
egrets in the shallows, and great blue herons
fishing, crook-necked: these are behind them, waiting.

Some maintain, when all of them give up watching,
they could see it clearly. I keep my silence,
knowing legend starts with uncertain visions.
Neither day nor hour is my way of waiting,
not the weary chase after revelation.
Red-winged blackbirds—those, I would stake my life on.

III

Front-Page Photograph: Memorial Day

Do-nothing day. Still-cool morning.
In bare feet on the concrete stoop,
I pick the paper up, uncurl it,

and see: before a grave's white cross,
(a phrase comes to me: *prostrate with grief*)
a woman lies face down in the grass,

forehead resting on folded arms.
I glance at the caption: fiancé.
And my thinking shifts, and my face warms—

the shoulders bare, the long legs parted:
the last embrace. Should I be seeing
this act of intimacy thwarted,

this woman-six-feet-above position?
Suddenly now I find myself
firing my hard, unanswered questions

at air, while a stubborn cardinal sings
his turf-war song like a car alarm
and flaps the bloody flag of his wings.

Ballade for the Last Move

Reject, discard: so much must go
to fit the more constrained designs
her living space will dwindle to.
And though the polished rosewood shines
where sun leaks through venetian blinds,
the moving crew will storm the door
too soon. She balks, resists, repines.
What comfort is she searching for?

China: twelve settings. Needed? No.
In fact, she never entertains.
The crystal never held bordeaux
or beaujolais; she knows no wines.
Her teacups keep their tight confines;
her silver cloisters in the drawer
in dust each grating minute grinds.
What graces was she searching for?

And nothings that she strains to know
the whys of keeping, and consigns
to closet shelves, too high, too low—
the broken books with torn-off spines,
the tchotchke china figurines—
they did mean something, once. They bore
some weight the chain of time unwinds,
some substance she was searching for.

I read her face between the lines.
Whatever current stirred her core
is neutral now behind her eyes.
What woman am I searching for?

Finding the Lego

You find it when you're tearing up your life,
trying to make some sense of the old messes,
moving dressers, peering under beds.
Almost lost in cat hair and in cobwebs,
in dust you vaguely know was once your skin,
it shows up, isolated, fragmentary.
A tidy little solid. Tractable.
Knobbed to be fitted in a lock-step pattern
with others. Plastic: red or blue or yellow.
Out of the dark, undamaged, there it is,
as bright and primary colored and foursquare
as the family with two parents and two children
who moved in twenty years ago in a dream.
It makes no allowances, concedes no failures,
admits no knowledge of a little girl
who glared through tears, rubbing her slapped cheek.
Rigidity is its essential trait.
Likely as not, you leave it where it was.

Saving the Appearances

Her body, at rest, tends to remain at rest
late, mornings. The warm hand on her breast
is gone now, like the rest of him, from bed,
transited out of view. Now, in her head,
theories glide in pavane. Datum: the way
his path of orbit strays, although today
damp sheets sigh fragrance here, where he was lying.
The loveliest of theories, always dying.
Phlogiston, say. The luminiferous aether.
The notion that they need not love each other
to own the darkness of this energy.
That only principled uncertainty
governs his loopy reappearances.
Perhaps he's like those fizzy bubble-dances,
those *tours en l'air* through Ptolemy's universe?
A pleasing scheme, but finally perverse.
The solar system is Copernican.
Her earth is not the focus, but his sun,
his flare and blaze the drivers of her moves,
old forces that no gravity reproves.
And somewhere in her mind a model shatters,
unstable at the core, because it matters
how little time or space they have remaining.
She sees, therefore, no method of attaining
unification of these fields of heart.
Once more the strings of theory fray apart.
Back to the data. Sort the facts afresh.
Neutrinos whistle through her naked flesh.

Weather Radio

*A special receiver for the continuous broadcasts of the
weather service, tuned to a noncommercial frequency and set
to sound an alert when hazardous weather is approaching.*

He, in love with certainty but uncertain,
reasoned they would need one in Minnesota.
She, blown back and forth by so many changes,
bent to his reasons,

torn like scattered cloud cover. Newly married—
too soon transferred out of the life that held them
tracked and steady, dropped in a different landscape
known for its dangers,

blown away—they'd veered from initial forecasts.
Heat-wave nights had simmered to dead-calm watches,
unexpected floods and subzero mornings.
Nervous, they bought one,

kitchen-counter almond, the little unit
squat and square. The National Weather Service,
voices bright and confident over breakfast,
taught them to settle

down to standard formats and scripted statements.
Over time, though fronts reappeared, and cloudbursts
kept their pattern, *safe* was the watchword, *safety*.
Whether they noticed

human voices gradually disappearing
(year on year, recordings and then computers),
speech did not yet seem to them wholly absent,
mostly synthetic.

Still, it sometimes rattled them how the warnings,
past now, blared alarms, how the hours that followed
beeped alerts, how poised over North Dakota
something was coming.

After the Divorce, I Hold a Yard Sale

They come in slowly, poker faced.
Such laying bare of earthly failings—
spread on folding tables, draped
on porch railings—

is sad and awkward, and they pass,
eyes down, before the bargain bins
and clothing racks that now confess
our venial sins:

the treadmill bought in a gust of hope
that fell, predictably, becalmed;
the set of free weights; the jump-rope,
plastic-embalmed—

enthusiasms failed. And Lord,
what hubris in these color schemes!
Which idiot was overfond
of whites and creams?

What germ of evil in our past
infected this computer's sheath,
once beige, now with a yellowish cast
like rotten teeth?

The screw loose and the weak-linked chain:
nothing in literature or art
so bluntly explicates the line
Things fall apart. . . .

They lie there derelict, unhaggled,
wasted, remaindered, on the skids,
redemptionless. But now a gaggle
of college kids

has blown in on a gale of laughter,
talking trash. May youth forgive
the faults age will no longer suffer!
May these bones live.

Light, Motif

June night. Light hangs late for us, porch-swing lazy.
Truck goes by with the windows open, spilling
blue notes, tenor saxophone line unwinding
into the twilight.

Corner. Turning. Gone.
                         But the world is altered
now, because those measures of hopeless longing
tumbled on us under this sky whose blue notes
lean into nighttime.

(Lolling summer, you with your long vacations,
lawns and pools and languorous blue-note evenings,
hear it? Here: your end, in a dying line of
saxophone solo.)

Maintenance Work

Start with the plain directions for the task
of puttying window frames: carry the tools
out to the summer lawn; for a moment, bask

in sideways-slanting sun. The dew's jewels,
set one per grass blade, Tiffany pavé,
could launch ten poems, but I stick to rules

and center my being on this work. I lay
one frame on the old sawhorses, pockmarked
with spatters of ancient paint. My job today:

to proof these storms against the evils worked
by northern winters, every element
of weather—and do it with my mind unforked.

The goal is contemplation: to be transparent,
be doing only that which I am doing,
be *now,* without distraction, in the moment—

just what my brain resists. It keeps pursuing
the tangents of things. The *now,* for one. *Maintenant*
pops in my head like a flashbulb, and *bang,* I'm reviewing

French etymology, thinking: it's from *tenant*
and *main;* it's like *holding in hand.* Understood:
It means grasping this *now* like a solid—just what I want.

Should I let this thought play out more fully? I could.
But I'll save that up for a *now* of writing, revising.
I straighten up, breathe, center again. The wood

is filled in where it was rotted; the loose glazing
is balanced woozily on new glazer's points.
I open the putty, scoop a glob, start squeezing.

Goosh: the putty between my fingers. Faint
chemical smells, and the *goosh,* and I'm gone, away.
A thousand miles and fifty years, at Saint . . .

Saint James's preschool, Arlington, VA.
I'm a concentrated knot of wonder, sitting
at a long, low table, gooshing modeling clay.

You see? I'm bad at this! The mind-moth, flitting
past every light bulb, wanton, never true,
needs cloistering. I straighten, breathe. Fitting

comes after squeezing: carefully prodding goo
against the glass and frame with a fingertip.
I take my time. The sun warms. Scraps of blue

blink sky-light through the maple. A fat strip
of putty lumped with fingertip indents
is in place at last. I'm *here, now,* but the grip

of presentness is weak. The shapes of the dents
and the scents and textures racket it off again
to pie crust, pastry, bread dough, the intense

muscle knowledge of kneading. To heck with Zen
for five seconds! I'm powerless faced with food.
But lunch is not yet, and I'm not sure when,

so I breathe, center. Focus on the wood.
Steady the knife against the frame, and pull
gently, planing the clay to a clean edge. Good.

And it comes to me that the *now* is not the dull
literal and empirically verifiable
now of the right-now hand and eye, but the whole

constellation of catch in the mind's nets, friable
clumps of realness squeezed to a different juice,
the meltdown of one to another by mind, the pliable

putty of sense in the fingers of mind. So I loose
my hold on the leash of wordplay and let it run,
and it veers from *maintenant* to *maintenance,* whose use

in modern English is upkeep, but here's the pun:
it's *tenant* again, and *main, holding* and *hand.*
To hold your wealth, hand-work it. Stand in the sun,

in the *now,* fixing your windows. It's a grand
satisfaction: putty ready for paint,
and a poem. Your *sensei* will understand.

Dutch Elm

That trees would die
yearly, we knew. The columns of the nave
of Summit Avenue, the architrave
of openwork where canopies unfold,
green or briefly gold,
the arched, leaf-dripping limbs
backlit with sky—

in every year, some go.
Some ends arrive with force: the papers warn
with pictures, after every storm,
of fallen branches, hollow at the heart,
or great trunks snapped apart,
battering cars and houses with the blows.
(We knew, but now we know.)

Some ends are quiet: the red
stripes appearing, like a garotting wound,
on trunks where the inspectors found
beetles in bark, bare limbs lurking in shade.
The tree crew and the chainsaw blade
will come—we know now—soon—
The stripe says, *This is dead.*

They make short work of things
with sweat and cherry pickers, saws and zeal,

rope and rappelling acrobatic skill
and limb-shredding machines.
Only the stump remains
and is soon sawdust: nothing left to chance
but next year's fairy rings.

No help for it, then.
This cut to sky, this coring of the heart.
These trees too far apart.
This just delivered balled-and-burlapped stick,
its trunk two inches thick,
decades from beauty. What we always knew:
we start again.

Preservation

What's wrenching is how utterly it's gone.
No cheers. Only the summer traffic noise
droning above White Castle's greasy litter.
The outfield wall—for years the last bit left
of the wooden ballpark—sulking at the back
of a rundown mall I struggle to remember?
It's nowhere now. A snip of guidebook prose
has leveled sixty years of minor leagues
to a modifier: "including *Lexington Park*
in the Midway district."

                       Gone, like so much else,
even the recollection of what's gone.
What filled that block downtown before the Dome?
When did they blast Met Stadium to powder?
The Kittson house? The U.S. Customs Building?
The streetcar tracks?

                     Perhaps this is a mercy.
Merciful, that we are not made to remember
(as you will remember, in a moment more)
all lost things. That not everything burns in
like the Murrah Federal Building, the Twin Towers,
or the kitchen fire in a Collegetown apartment.
A mercy, when no monuments polish pain
or bind it, like a sword, with spell and ritual,
inside a stone, or seal it in airless glass
with the safe and sacred text of exhibitions.

I know, I know this way is merciful
as I stand hatless in hard vacation sunshine
in a place I have not stood for thirty years,
a place I no longer know except by street signs.
And so the journey was pointless. And so the children,
who knew from the start it was someone else's journey,
are bored, and whining to go to Valleyfair.

Feast of Corpus Christi

Grow up here and you learn that God is insatiable:
God will consume you. You learn this best from the sky.
Two hours' drive from the Cities, the clutter of suburb
drops away like pretense, and then: that sky,
unbroken from one horizon to the other
over the corn and soybeans, the soybeans and corn.
The bowl of sky, scooped out, from the June sunrise
in a ribbon of molten gold at one edge of the world
to the place where night presses blue into black.
Those ends of the earth. You learn from seeing them
in the school ballfield, setting up chairs with your father.
Everything open, taking whatever comes,
the doors of the church, the gaps in the ragged procession.
Even the dead teach you, their monuments
in the churchyard—saints, Virgins—patient, unmoved,
while children walk in a line before the priest
sweltering in his vestments, lifting the monstrance.
The altar boys sweating, suffering all for God.
The church supper for His glory. The cloudless sky.

Swing

Memory held in suspension: the swing in the summer,
hanging on chains from the beadboard, the double-hung windows
open around it. The three-season porch and the swing

where we rocked and read, rocked and reread the stories,
the piles of library books about Chincoteague ponies,
filled with cloud-dark magic, their large illustrations

dazing your head as my voice rode upward and downward,
rising and falling in waves, like the thunderheads rolling
in from the north, the coal-black stallions of cloud—

swinging still, though we smelled the storm on the doorstep
and watched the droplets, their heaviness shaking the buds
of trumpet-vine blooms (their lipstick coral, their fragrance),

felt the air cooling, heard the hooves of the raindrops,
muffled our ears to the blowing in of the autumn
over and over, suspending ourselves in the story.

IV

Incident Report

Naïve, you're thinking. *Soft.*
You want my story pre-packaged.
Hard-coded. As in BURGLRY
or RBRY, ARMD, OF PRSN.
But how do I code this hardness?
In the cramped back of the bus
one girl, for no cause I can see,
barks at another: *HO.*
Hisses *Need to be SMACKED,*
marking the word with a clap
that knifes the air, heavy
between the side-facing seats
where we tense, trapped, quiet,
skin sweat-glued to plastic.
Now on her feet, as if
to get off—to make for the exit
along with her posse of rowdies—
she flashes a fake-nailed hand.
It drops like a bomb, bursting
against the rouge-pink cheek.
The whack of it: then chaos.
The rowdies cackle; they bolt;
the slapped girl reddens; she cowers,
fingering stripes of welt.
We pelt her with scattered shock—
words like *assault* and *report*—

but her face crumples to tears.
In an angry fumble of jacket
and backpack, she staggers off
at Marion and Ravoux.

See, I have filled out the form
on the hard lines of your silence.

Viva Voce

Listen: her voice, did you hear? The support that she gives her contralto,
focusing sound in the mask of the face, in the resonant chambers
combing the skull, in the lips—if I think of it hard I can feel it
still, my old voice teacher crying for *resonance*—oh, and she has it!
Years ago, *I* used to have it—

Marshall and Snelling, she chants to us. Not every bus driver calls them,
the names of the streets, but this one is vain of her voice, and with reason.
Yes, I can easily see it: she stood at some teacher's piano
learning the pull of the muscles, stretching a line from the cheekbones,
soft palate lifting in secret—

Snelling and West University. Not a poetic recital.
Was there a vocal career that died at its birth or before it?
Does she resent it, that all she intones is mundane information?
Nothing inspiring, except in the way she takes pains to express it,
placing the consonants crisply,

fearful, perhaps, for the role of the warm, living folds of the larynx
nowadays. So many beautiful digital voices around us!
Everywhere, feminine voices. They tell us that trains are arriving,
leaving, or closing their doors, in sultry and come-hither mezzos,
lulling us into believing,

guiding with gentle persuasion through mazes of telephone menus.
(Somewhere I heard: in Japan, the mellifluous voice is soprano,
floating above the cacophony, breathing *Please exit the building;
it is on fire.*) They surround us, the bodiless sirens of safety.
Think of the meaning behind them:

no one is there who can hear you. Listen: the powdery static
of cell phones, their petulant ringing. Someone is making a phone call,
hearing the jingly recording—overly cheerful, too lilting—
telling him no one will answer. Stuffing the phone in his pocket.
Cursing the hollowed-out heart of it—

Lake and Fourteenth. There she is again, waking me out of my musings,
daydreaming fears of my cricket-voice chirping its warnings unanswered.
Praise for her singing alive, for her voice and her ears that can hear me
voicing my thanks for the song, for the singer, the muse, and the bus route.
Sing to me: *Lake and Chicago.*

Two Funerals

Pass them. You must. Dark-uniformed, sharp-creased—

the whole force here. No squads to cruise up East,

Their stiff, flag-bearing ranks strand toward the hill

to work the trash-pocked site of that soured drug deal

near the cathedral. Pass, in the midst of badges

where chaos blasted and bled from weekend grudges

and guns? You must. You must: you are called to sing,

into this grief, this grace-and-gospel wailing,

to wring from air high-chanted ceremonies,

where young men hug, grim faced, and lower their eyes,

numb, while priests and politicians speak

to their own open graves, next month, next week—

O hard recessional hymn where no one touches!

File past the suit-clean body, the casket's satin ruches.

In one patrolman's hands, the rosewood box of ashes.

Late Season Day Trip

Because it could only happen in summer, because
an early start was vital, because we'd run
outside in the grass by the driveway, our sneakers wet,
the air still cool, so early the light went sideways,
because it changed things, because we would be saved
by water from our humid suburban sins,

because we'd begin by driving into the sun,
in oriente, compass point of the pilgrim,
past New Life Church and Transformation Salon
and PMZ Plasma Services, where debt
is washed away in blood, because of hope,

because each year we forgot the hard returning
until it came, the late-night driving back
on the black, unbending highways, the cranky children,
forgot the trash on the seats, forgot the way
we steeled ourselves for the dark and the year's forgetting,

all this is why I can bear to stand on a corner
a thousand miles from the shore, in a second-hand suit,
and wait alone for a bus that will take me to work,
watching others leave at the end of summer,
the early sunlight barreling like a truck
down east-west streets, and the gulls of parking lots
wheeling in carnival arcs, screaming the sea.

Chiller

Seven a.m. The hunter's moon
a scarface falling down the sky
in knife-edge dark. A siren sounds
its bad-suspense-film leitmotif.
In porch light on the paving stones,
trench-coated for my working life,
I pull the doorknob (opening scene,
take twenty thousand), turn the key.
The dead hand of a pin-oak leaf
crabwalks across the alleyway.

Soundtrack

The movies lied. No trumpets stormed the gate
of change. No modulation cued a shiver.
No Foley artist paused to isolate
a postman's footsteps, trudging to deliver
the future, with a form for her to sign.
No hand-held-camera close-up framed the word
crisis over a weeping oboe line.
No. On the sunlit sidewalk, all she'd heard
was life: his work-sounds, high in the maple tree
in flawless autumn; starlings in the eaves;
rakes on the pavement; gusts of garden chat.
The present, humming absentmindedly.
One crack. Then, in a crush of twigs and leaves,
one cry. The white noise roaring after that.

Layover

Attention passengers: Flight 1491 has been canceled. . . .

Note to self: *the middle of the journey.*
That's all that's needed. No *dark wood* required.

Notice the colors: how they're like fine ash,
a universe already burned to cinders.
Walls, floors, furniture, signs, everything visible:
a pall of pale gray, bone white.

                         Look at the faces—
when you can see them, when you're not in a line,
your knuckles clenched on the handle of your carry-on—
the hard set of the mouths, the downturned eyebrows.

Hear the bodies speak: the ache of muscles
slouched in fatigue on unforgiving plastic.
No other speech. Recall a definition
of hell: to be alone with one's private rage.

Be vigilant. Keep listening for the agent,
there at the narrow gate, and for some word
about another flight, an open seat,
some unexpected mercy. Strike from your mind
that line about abandoning every hope.

Epistle to the Pumpkin Field

This is the truth:
they knife your face,

drag out your entrails
to feed to the crows,

and set the flame
in what remains.

Ecstatic vision.
One night: you shine.

A Choral Service for All Souls

Tomás Luis de Victoria, 1603

Needle-lace of sound,
bright mesh drawn taut by death, enclosing
Requiem's plain ground,
damask patterns in lament
that thin or open, here, or here, exposing
each line's luminous ornament—

or should I say the death-melisma winds
among these glitterings of spark,
a thorn-and-briar stem?
Or grows its bones inside the moving limbs,
memento mori stiffening them?

Either way, what drives this is the dark:

the mezzo voices' cantus line.
The plaint of plainsong, keening under all.
While dissonances shift, evolve,
around the straight tone's subtly bending spine,

it stands. I feel the major chords resolve.
The hands fall.

Portent

What does it mean?
To wake in the dark from a dream of Balanchine

where the strings speak
tight-throated chords, passionate but oblique,

and on stage, stark,
upright, slow as the mast of a distant bark,

the ballerina drifts
up the diagonal, two partners lifting

the pillared form, pointe shoes shoulder-high—
a standard drawn across a bloodied sky.

They bear her away from me.

How do I know this isn't victory?

Phone Call, 6:00 A.M.

"If you believe," he shouted to them, "clap your hands. . . ."
— J.M. Barrie, Peter Pan

The twinkling in the dark is Tinkerbell.
She's dying. We must clap to make her well.
I'll find my hands now—
                                    No. Wake up. Your cell

is blaring at you, beaming your sister's name.
(Whack of adrenaline that strikes you dumb.)
Except that can't be true. A call from home—

oh. Her husband, needing to confer
about the last arrangements. Speak now. Stir
your thick tongue past her name, her absence, her,

gone, like a nova flared against the night,
pulsing to signal that some sickened light
died centuries ago. It is too late,

a simple fact your cell phone fails to mark.
It still believes. You keep it in the dark.

Notes

"Confessional Work: Late Advent": *Rorate coeli,* "Drop down dew, ye heavens," a chant sung during Advent. *The prayer of another season: white as snow:* from Psalm 51, sung during Lent.

"Cold Case": The riddle's solution is "window frost."

"Vintage Pattern": *Simplicity* is a manufacturer of sewing patterns.

"Mayday": *who let the ground give way/ in Port-au-Prince* is a reference to the Haiti earthquake of 2010.

Maryann Corbett grew up in McLean, Virginia. She holds a doctorate in English from the University of Minnesota and is the author of *Breath Control* (David Robert Books, 2012), and the chapbooks *Gardening in a Time of War* (Pudding House) and *Dissonance* (Scienter Press). Her poems, essays, and translations have appeared in *River Styx, Atlanta Review, Rattle* e-issues, *The Evansville Review, Measure, Literary Imagination, The Dark Horse, Mezzo Cammin, Linebreak, Subtropics,* and many other journals in print and online, as well as the anthologies *Hot Sonnets, Able Muse Anthology,* and *Imago Dei: Poems from Christianity and Literature.* Her poems have been finalists for Best of the Net and the Morton Marr Prize and have won the Lyric Memorial Award and the Willis Barnstone Translation Prize. She lives in Saint Paul, Minnesota, and works for the Minnesota Legislature. She is married to John Corbett, a teacher of statistics and mathematics, and they have two grown children.

Credo for the Checkout Line in Winter was a finalist for the Able Muse Book Award in 2011.

ALSO FROM ABLE MUSE PRESS

Ben Berman, *Strange Borderlands - Poems*

Michael Cantor, *Life in the Second Circle - Poems*

Catherine Chandler, *Lines of Flight - Poems*

Margaret Ann Griffiths, *Grasshopper - The Poetry of M A Griffiths*

April Lindner, *This Bed Our Bodies Shaped - Poems*

Frank Osen, *Virtue, Big as Sin - Poems*

Alexander Pepple (Editor), *Able Muse Anthology*

Alexander Pepple (Editor), *Able Muse - a review of poetry, prose & art* (semiannual issues, Winter 2010 onward)

James Pollock, *Sailing to Babylon - Poems*

Aaron Poochigian, *The Cosmic Purr - Poems*

Hollis Seamon, *Corporeality - Stories*

Matthew Buckley Smith, *Dirge for an Imaginary World - Poems*

Wendy Videlock, *The Dark Gnu and Other Poems*

Wendy Videlock, *Nevertheless - Poems*

Richard Wakefield, *A Vertical Mile - Poems*

www.ablemusepress.com

www.ingramcontent.com/pod-product-compliance
Lightning Source LLC
Chambersburg PA
CBHW021409090426
42742CB00009B/1076